Side by Side

Written by Keith Pigdon
Series Consultant: Linda Hoyt

WorldWise
Content-based Learning

Contents

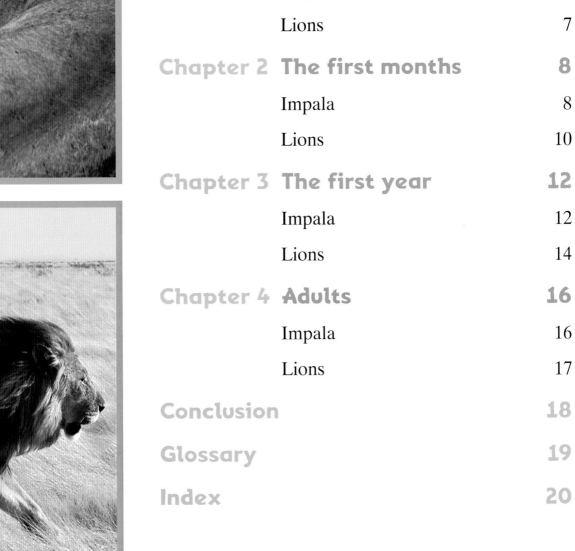

Introduction

Lions and impala live close to each other on the grasslands of Africa. They share the same **habitat**.

Impala eat grass; the lions are powerful hunters and try to eat impala, but impala are well **adapted** for life among **predators**.

Which animal has the best chance of surviving?

CHAPTER 1

Birth

Impala

An impala **fawn** grows inside its mother for about 200 days.

The fawn is born in the middle of the day when **predators** like lions are resting. A mother usually gives birth to one fawn at a time.

The newborn impala is very strong and weighs about five kilograms. It can stand up ten minutes after it is born.

A newborn impala fawn with its mother.

A newborn lion cub with its mother.

Lions

Lion cubs grow inside their mother for about 110 days.

The cubs are born in a safe place under a bush or among rocks. Up to four cubs may be born at the same time.

When they are born, lion cubs usually weigh about one kilogram. They are blind and helpless.

CHAPTER 2

The first months

Impala

Forty minutes after it is born, an impala **fawn** can follow its mother. The mother licks the fawn all over to get rid of any smells that might attract predators.

The fawn feeds on its mother's milk. When the mother leaves the fawn to **graze**, the fawn hides in the grass until she returns. The mother watches carefully for **predators** before she returns to her young.

Find out more

How do newborn impala survive the first months of life?

8

Impala drink milk from their mothers soon after they are born.

Lions

The lion cubs stay hidden for the first months of their lives. Their mother picks them up in her mouth and moves them from hiding place to hiding place. She leaves them in that safe spot while she hunts for food.

She needs to eat a lot of food so she can produce enough milk for her cubs. The cubs try hard to get plenty of milk. Cubs that do not get enough milk are weaker than the others and are less likely to live.

Lion cubs drink milk from their mothers soon after they are born.

Lions carry their young in their mouths.

CHAPTER 3

The first year

Impala

After three months, young impala are strong enough to keep up with the herd. The herd helps protect them from attacks by **predators**.

After five months, the **fawns** stop drinking their mothers' milk and **graze** with the adult impala.

Half of all impala die before they are one year old.

The herd helps protect young impala from predators.

Lions

After three months, the lion cubs can follow their mothers. Together, they join a family group called a pride. A pride may have as many as 40 lions or as few as ten. The pride includes the male lions that are the fathers of the cubs.

The adults in the pride help protect the cubs from predators. Sometimes male lions, that do not belong to the pride, challenge the male lions that do belong in the pride. If these new male lions do take over the pride, they kill any cub that does not belong to them.

Lion cubs cannot survive on their own until they are two years old. Eight out of ten cubs die in their first year.

The pride helps protect young lions from predators.

CHAPTER 4

Adults

Impala

By the time impala are one year old, they are adults.

Adult impala can run at 80 kilometres per hour. Their long legs help them to reach top speed in tall grass. They can leap long distances and can jump very high.

An adult impala chased by an adult lion will usually get away.

Adult impala can jump very high.

?

Did you know?

Impala can travel almost nine metres in one leap. They can jump three metres high.

16

Adult lions stalk their prey.

Lions

Lions are adults by the time they are three or four years old. They learn to hunt by watching the older members of the pride.

Adult lions can reach a speed of 56 kilometres per hour, but they cannot run as fast as their **prey**. When chasing prey through long grass, lions find it hard to reach top speed. A pride of lions usually hunts together by **stalking** its prey.

17

Conclusion

Impala are well **adapted** for life on the African grasslands, where they live among lions and other **predators**.

Impala **fawns** are stronger and less helpless at birth than lion cubs. They learn to look after themselves and become adults faster than lion cubs. They can run fast enough in the long grass to escape when lions are chasing them.

Although lions are skilled and powerful hunters, they have less chance of survival than impala.

Glossary

adapted   when a living thing has changed so that it exists in its environment better

fawn   a young animal such as a young deer, antelope or impala

graze   to eat grass or other plants

habitat   the place where a plant or an animal naturally lives

predators   animals that get food by killing and eating other animals

prey   an animal that is caught and eaten by another animal

stalking   sneaking up slowly and quietly behind their prey when hunting

Index